king's(mère)

king's(mère)

or the book of

by

Nathan Dueck

TURNSTONE PRESS

king's(mère)

Turnstone Press
Artspace Building
607-100 Arthur Street
Winnipeg, MB
R3B 1H3 Canada
www.TurnstonePress.com

Turnstone Press gratefully acknowledges the assistance of The Canada Council for the Arts, the Manitoba Arts Council, the Government of Canada through the Book Publishing Industry Development Program and the Government of Manitoba through the Department of Culture, Heritage and Tourism, Arts Branch, for our publishing activities.

The Canada Council for the Arts | Le Conseil des Arts du Canada

Manitoba Arts Council | Conseil des arts du Manitoba

Canada

Cover design: Tétro Design
Interior design: Sharon Caseburg

Printed and bound in Canada by Friesens for Turnstone Press.

National Library of Canada Cataloguing in Publication Data

Dueck, Nathan, 1979-

King's(mère) / Nathan Dueck.

Poems.
ISBN 0-88801-290-X

1. King, William Lyon Mackenzie, 1874-1950—Poetry. I. Title.

PS8557.U28145K55 2003 C811'.6 C2003-906487-5

pour
ma mère
& my father

king's(mère)

THIS BOOK has been chosen as the second to be dis-tributed to the Booklovers of the CARILLON BOOK CLUB of Canada.

This is copy
No ....
And is the Property of
....
....
....

Since his death, the Right Honourable W.L. Mackenzie King's writings have been exposed for all of Canada to read. Having lived a long life, having written many verses, King left many versions of himself. Herein is one such testament, the book of king's(mère)

the

theory;

or why

do I bother you? Let's assume King foresaw his end and composed this liturgy. Perhaps ours is a man humming a hymn before drifting off on his deathbed. Perhaps it is my own decomposition. Past editions have altered King's nearly illegible shorthand, nonstandard spellings, and poetic prose style. I've retained all such variations. (For instance, of that which follows, twohundredeightysix times do these letters form the word 'and' (and its derivation, 'ampers&')). Given so many variants and supplements, it is likely King himself would not recognize or even lay claim to the ruins that remain. Please consider this his vision, in the occult sense of the word, and humour him until the end. Were King to be resurrected and read the dogeared book you now hold, I would similarly ask for his patience. He would likely tattle on me to his ma. Notwithstanding, the King is dead, long live the King.

Monday, October 2, 1893.

(Handwritten)

Wrote a letter & a short poem before going to bed last night.

She was a widow under glass framed by a window. King wrote of looking at her through the book open to the hills of her lap. The sun's tongue dawned on her and blinded me.
I, his unknown, unseen, eye.

septemberfiftheighteenninetythree

'The foregoing generations beheld God and nature face to face;
we, through their eyes.'

Ralph Waldo Emerson

MR. WILLIAM LYON MACKENZIE KING'S (1874-1950)

DIARIES, correspondence, & *SCRIPTURE.*

published according to the true original copies

A King may not marry (in order of appearance).

Dear little Mother.	Isabel King.
(by right of ascending line).	
Mirror.	eyes
Self.	Rex.
(the equal collateral line).	
Dearest companion.	Pat.
Ladies & other ne'er do wells.	Madonna?
Picture window mistress.	Belle.
(the unequal collateral line).	
son	
(the right descending line).	

Printed in TORONTO 1947.

Mother:

Am your little Willie daydreaming under noon-beams of light, birds, & you.

To Belle:

Enjoyed seeing you 'n the morning. I promise you only a true & loving heart, a sincere & lasting devotion, a never-failing but an ever increasing love. Muses didn't abuse me before you.

I am a bestman standing aside the wedding. A witness to the sunburnt bouquet. I am sand melting hour by hour.

The Book of
Kingsmère

CHAPTER 1

AND King said unto those of the second war committee that he would not increase the numbers of the sixth division as a warning to the Army that the nation would revolt under King's reign.

2 For it came that his beloved and dearest companion Pat neared passing. Yet this forthcoming death would not likewise bury King's lands. And King said: 'Thus saith the LORD God of Canada. The sun has set over the people of the lake, and those looking into these waters.

4 I know thy time and its meaning unto me. My people have fallen, as my watch from my pocket, at the evening hour of ten and five. Here I write in the poor light of thy patience, and thy works great spirits; and you, precious little Pat, shall be first among equals.

5 "God will be with you till we meet again".

Pat, I pour out in writing unto thee, until mourning, messages dyed in love to deliver forth to mother, as this your passing evokes the sorrow of another so long ago; those lovely Belles that once were the mirror of my envy; and father, that which I will never be as your leaving will leave me a son deprived of a son for his throne.

6 Day passes and I read and rest as one son of those who bore me. I recall when mother passed to sleep with the fathers. Welcome God spirit of Pat.'

CHAPTER 16

31 You have been that with which I pain and concern myself, and that which I have sought for companionship. I see my reward through your window of suffering. As I found in my mother.

30 Here I read the words unto thee that have burned my soul at noonday. It is my love; it is written and partly unwritten:

ashamed
to record it all

(write it daily wt. frailty
& become purer in thought
& word
& act)

Saw the lady in the berth
below making her toilet.

two trolls on the town
stroll down on to it
few belles, sigh
'‘s that all
you've got'

In a cup of spirit
I saw eyes
I saw her
finger wt. mine
a round band bound
King & this belle

(oh how Hell's
chains bear on a man
faltering.)

I saw her close,
the light on her lip
becoming cheeky.

No man or onanist
has ever
known this lady

To do the big work
of the nation I feel I
should be married.

'see men
sink down the
hole'

HEARKEN BACK

by CLAIRE VOYANT

A politician, Willy King was quick to learn the art of double talk. In his first election bid as official opposition leader, his forked tongue licked many ballot boxes.

* * *

VOTERS heard word that, 'He is 33 years old and a drop of liquor has never passed his lips'. In dry mouths, the phrase was of total teetotaller. To the others, the bottle whetted Willy's insatiable appetite.

ring,
I should have,
knocked up, rang
ladies long ago
(my Jezebel & I whining
a little time together
a little hymn & a little prayer

three
shillings, an angel
& half bottle of wine)
saddened I,
a little Willie, came

Lady:
you saw me &
you gave me
swollen eyes

(& they told me
I could never keep a diary)

king me

(Handwritten)

This morning I purchased 5 tickets for 'Antigone'. I started down town to King St., went upstairs & asked for my Miss Bella. She was in & came 'n to her room & spoke to me. We had a long & beautiful talk. Poor girl cried a great deal & promised to leave the life she was leading right there & then to come 'n from where she was.

Had Pillow Fight with Billy King

Mrs. Belladonna remembers attending a children's party at 'Woodside' and spending the night there.

She slept in 'the same bed as Billy'. She recalls a rather spirited 'pillow fight' with the future prime minister before retiring.

Which King Ruled the Throne?

My mind wanders while wondering about the influence Isabel Grace King had on the development of her son, W.L. Mackenzie King.

Historically, the boy eliminated right next to where he slept. Willy's sleeping quarters were directly behind the family's washroom, separating his parents' room from the family 'throne' (forgetting each member's piss-pot).

left a paper tr a i l meant one day to tell her

'Excuse me, man. May I ask what your idea of duty is?'

excuse me

'I'm losing patience. A son's duty to his mother.'

sir (i) deliver mail (i) don't kno—

'Not duty, she is the purest & sweetest soul that God had ever made.'

certainly may (i) now complete my route

'You will not sully my dear little mother.'

listen king (i) send these letters wherever (i) please

Willie wrung words out to fill her slit. A mailman turned into Woodside, as he did every day. A mailman wrote letters at the bottom of his page and rang her bell.

a mailman said
reading will make king cross

oh lifeeffigy it does not
become changed in a spell
oh God, o god, ohgod
where! where! where! What!
oh what! oh what!
o miserable man that I am,
what sort of pawn am I?

To take a queen in one move.
said

Where as typewriting sounds like kissing, longhand does not. A mute amusement she was. Call I hope he—

Ah, I saw christ
in the painting over her
bed to be a
'strong son of God'
that is my mission.
To reveal christ
in public life & service.

typeface looks like pools of arches and spots and dotted (i)s
you said

I enter. (I
have seen very little
of her to-day).

To-day:
            I happened to engage
wt. nine men
One of them
  Said 'eyes were
  bigger than my stomach'
  & meant 'mouth'.
Hypocrite
  plays fast & loose
  preys on lack of
  resolution.
Covered face wt.
  wine lees
 (why?
   never the less).
Denied prayer
sat under grand eloquent
  tree of ignorance.
Watched but didn't
  greet.

holy fool
confessed in her frame

Looked through the glass whl. writing the last line. See the small bird fly into your window. Thinking of someone he longs to build a home with in heaven.

I kiss your hand,

King

Adversary, you plucked quills and inked desire. I, sired. Defeat us.
Adulteress. You flightless bird. Pray forgiveness, my prey

In plain words
an angel (sounds
angelus) effaces
my anatomy
(in me the sky
is falling).

(left me
reciting vows)

We wt. glass eyes
& arttragicomedy
& stones)

My transparent eye
ball swam, saw
particles of God in
her privates & in
his testicles.

Vision splendid .men shall have Dominion from sea to see

'I remember seeing him walking into church, silk hat and cape and his little mother proudly on his arm. When they got to church ushers showed them a place of prominence.'

Verheiratet.

On 12 December, in the bride's mother's house in Toronto, by Rev. A. Topp, John King, lawyer of Berlin, and Isabella Grace, youngest daughter of William Lyon Mackenzie.

Berliner Journal 19 December 1875

Mary & John could not agree
Quarrelled with pertinacity
Neighbours said, 'What a cruel thing';
And sent for Lyon Mackenzie King

"Official Umpire"

He gave voice to an apparition. A grave voice, gravelly with might. Femalevolence.

the photos in
low neck.
I don't care
for them at all (didn't want that
sort of socket
of ether).

The photograph below was taken on a tour of the Mackenzie King house. You can see (upper left) a white haze drooping. It is ectoplasm bringing in the spirit of King.

King's Birthplace Rests in Pieces?

by ABRAHAM ELL

A red-brick Pentecostal Tabernacle stands solemnly on the plot where Mackenzie King grew up.

On March 1926, without fanfare or commentary, a white frame house where the future Prime Minister was born was torn down.

To our collective shame, Kitchener has never made any money or monument to the fallen King castle.

* * *

WOODSIDE'S setting has sent shivers up and down the spines of many generations. In light of King's interest in mysticism and spiritualism, our superstitions may not have simply been old wives' tales.

Mum's the word.

1917.

I tell you this for its importance. I say, Belle King. She has engaged in behaviour not befitting my status. I have so many last words to share with you, my child.

Your letter is beautiful. It took me to a sort of Elysian field. They tell me in the war boys long for their mothers in the last minutes they draw breath. Well, I saw you in the trench the other day and you were comforted in water but you coughed with fever. I heard you say you were a 'male bound by . . . mmm . . . Biblical' meaning. I think you said. I understood, then, but now when I write I can only hear you tapping. I meant to tell you, they tapped me and quarts ran yellow out of my side. Nothing too good for my Rexy King.

I never knew why you were called Rex. I expect you would have told me if it were exciting.

How he came to be called Rex.

told to belle

We walked along streets of sin wt. many ladies & other ne'er do wells. I am glad I no longer find joy in such gatherings. My alma maters & I travelled along tipping the bottle for lost brothers. An unapologetic fellow, one of the devil's minions, meanders up & wrecks our tea. Emboldened, I thunder. After the incident the gentleman remarks that I seemed carnivorous to him. A tyrannosaurus said he.

in correspondence

Rex is not me. I do not even know the name. Returning home from a visit abroad my sister chose the name. A name from some Greek character to whom they claimed I bore likeness. How they knew about this Rex or how he looked I will never know nor they either. The name bereaves me though, for it betrays the Christian sense of purpose mother had in naming me after great-grandfather.

on a line of his diary

Father graduated from the University of Toronto. How was I, newly arrived, to know he had been dubbed 'Senator Rex'? I mentioned my father to The Varsity boys and referred to Kitchener (my birthplace, formerly Berlin) Ontario. It is a pseudonym of a former self.

I have just reworded my miserable little 'poem' 'The Crown of Thorns'. The Varsity's ass. editor Stephen Leacock (read: leaky cock) was correct. It is five verses of hardly literary rot.

~~Cockily~~ colicky, silently slides down
Raw shades of flowery ~~lifeless~~ Jesus. Aroused

Thro' ghosts of fifteen years,
Arisen here enwrapped in thee
By & by, beyond, the infected veil.
Mortalist woman un~~der~~earth ~~birthed~~
Passed stripped, soulless, & wt.ot. train.
I had someone to suckle, love.
There thou dost lie, & I
Sing over these little songs.

Imitation is suicide. Scale the cross while choking hemlock.

B - I - double L - Y K - I - N - G, BILLY KING
Proud of all the fighting all the fighting blood that's in him,
Never a word men can say again' him
B - I - double L - Y K - I - N - G KING
A name no shame has been connected with,
BILLY KING
THAT'S HIM

Will never forget
our cockeyed romance.
It was a bit of
true poetry.

I'm a proud lion
that I might not
die a virgin King.

I leave your
forehead in the breech.
Peasant.

THE LOVE OF MOTHERS

IN love for mothers human nature manifests its highest expression. It is the quality of soul by which, in his relations with his fellows, a son's capacity for service is determined; it is the fount at which all the finer springs of action are fed. Generosity, mercy, pity, friendship, devotion, sacrifice, flow from this one source, which conscious or unconscious borrowing can never exhaust.

The Secret of Heroism p. 78

CHAPTER 16

The message to the church at Abbey ruins

33 And unto the angel of this church it has been revealed that the Rex, son of Rex did evil in the sight of the almighty above all that were before him.

32 And it came to pass, as if it had been a light thing for Rex to weep black tears as rivers through his darkened ruins, that he took Jezebel as his wife and served Baal and worshipped him.

31 And she reared up an altar for Baal in the house of Baal which she had built in pictures. Jezebel spake unto Rex and calleth herself as his prophetess mother.

30 This raised up Rex's ear and he took his wife as the servant of Baal and formed a mirror of her wanting for her to mother a son. In her bosom they reflected as a mother and son together in unity as one.

29 And Baal read this doctrine of sin in the faces of the sinners and recalled his own falling and became sore jealous.

28 Through Rex's praises, Baal made himself a man with eyes as a flame of fire and feet as fine glass and entered Rex's home and saith:

27 As Jezebel lay with Rex as a martyr to his fatal lust, she will lie with me and I with her.

26 Rex had called in haste to Baal, as man, as to whether he had with Jezebel likened unto the picture. And Baal rose as the morning star within Jezebel and entered as with Rex's fathers.

27 And Jezebel came, after the hour of her temptation, and Rex girded up his loins and saith:

26 Thou hast known Baal and his unholy communication.

25 Take the cup of thine and pour it upon thy head in remembrance and say, Thus saith the LORD, I have anointed thee for Baal. Then open the door and the dogs shall overtake thee and eat thee, Jezebel, and there shall be none to bury thee.

24 And Rex opened the door and fled to lie with those before her.

<table>
<tr><td>lock my window
pane when reading
aloud letters to
belle
for you do not
want me to reflect
king
to ballpointpen
her image</td><td>lock her window
pain when read
my letters to you
isabel
mail
reflects belles
of the ball in mrs
king when
penetrated</td></tr>
<tr><td>Bell. Sound of glass</td><td>vinostainring</td></tr>
<tr><td>isabel let the mailman in</td><td>'You're on this side . . .
through the window'</td></tr>
</table>

a malaise
mother? my belle?
la belle hells'
without mercy
this mailman
whore son
rise sun
her(i)son
rex within
earshot up
humped
like dogs
he feared
on his
route

left her at the witching hour
stand guard of ~~is~~is
abel's woodside home cain
t wait with bells on

period

His feverous letters.

Here I lay & think well of you. Any bell is a belle. Do not lap their leg swill. & we enter the space before sunrise. In heat. & your oil-painted eyes follow. I collect eyes. I lie in writing & caress the man in the mirror where you most resemble her

.iiiiiiiiiiiiii

ps

kings writing is
bliss

-- March 1897

Mother Isabel,

(To go into politics with ot. marrying would be pure folly.) I am convinced that only the angels have kept me from falling. As I recover from this illness, prostrate with grief, there is a nurse who seems to possess such a beautiful Christian character & is constantly on my mind. She wears white & cleans my toilet. I'm shaving the hair of the dog, ma, from down there.

I believe the doggy in the window sent me this fever.

Daily I cover myself wt. another page & pour more ink upon myself. I see a symmetry. Can see God's reflection in dog. Such trifles inflame my nerves. But they all disappear & I find myself clasping your letters.

I look, as I have looked, for a wife. Or is it waif?

Little Willie

Forget his story.

(Typewritten)

If in the balance sheet of Life there be but left to my account a teardrop banished from some infant's eye, a smile created on some pale pinched jowl, a wrinkle smoothed in a furrowed brow, then, oh then I will have gained full all that I have ever given & leave the weary world with a happiness which passes all understanding.

PREFACE
The message of the carillon is a message of peace and good-will. Some of its notes will, I believe, be found in each of the sections which go to make up the pages of this book. The writings themselves are on a variety of topics, and have been made at different times. The *motif* of all is, however, the same.
W. L. MACKENZIE KING.

(a mailman cannot embellish letters or lie)
do not shoot the messenger
from st paul's hospital
to queen lay us

Mother——,

Ill from filthy water. Upon this pillow words flow—no, that's what they don't want me to say. They say that these letters are vital to survival & recovery. Phrenologists claim that a proper brain thrives on conjugality.

See a golden flower strain toward the sun. Branches blaze, love. Let the sun in.

Typhoid fever, cursed plague, Laodicians me when I write. Don't curse William, conquer. I wave my pen thro' the flames. My paltry ~~poultry~~ poetry, a poultice 'nder the evil influence.

Mother my nurse wld. like you. She is interested in human life, in saving man, thro' the betterment of conditions for the poor in spirit. She is a ray of light betwixt tulips. She is wholly virgin. I christen her M.ary.

~~This morning miss M came on duty.~~ ~~I have seen what is noblest & best in woman.~~

By birth bonds,

Willie King

Thou tire I see. Ah, yes. Why art thou gazing at thyself so?
Narcissus pleasured self-polluted palms. Aright thyself, go.

I am
still the child
tied by
an umbi
lical chord
a third leg
& apron strings.

(She no
urishes me)

Very wearied
but that is nothing.

Pound for pound,
measure for measure
eye for

One more lesson
not to put your
trust in anyone
under the sun.

prophesy

x'd eyes
i sphinx

goddessem
term
inated
on a
knee, gaited
easily

damned
without
out out
M.
or
elles'

Awaiting the turn of the century, Willy developed an aversion to clock chimes and looking glass. Rex wrote Queen Isabel from the hospital. I broke his wine-pressed Royal seal.

pass i on coats my hand my upturned palm lithe caresses
lethe streams

She is my nurse.
Yet, no love is like mother love.

his nurse wrote

[I veil King (the patient)'s words to Isabel (the patient's mother). For one devoted to cleanliness, or Godliness, such as I, it is a hard practice. Sterilize a patient's mind, unbeknownst to him. ~~It is an affair I temper with care.~~ You, mother, reply to me, the unknown. Please. ~~His recovery~~]

isabel knells: caught him in the act of self abuse and said 'Willie!' Caught him again. He must love the sound of his name.

Oh God make me
yours.
& humble
very humble.
I stumble. Make me
hum M. belle
me mum

Special, Ladies
"God's will, His will .... curses all who
Will's God, He will bless them who cuss Him best."

[please note: the patient's delayed maturation masks his potential for recovery. St. Paul's.]

Dated March 1897.
To Saint Paul's Hospital,

Given your statement I must suppose you seek to destroy the germs of dis-ease through the process I believe you call eugenics. Certainly, you did not read my concern for Willy to imply compliance with the death of Lord God's holy holy holy children. They are born into sin, not of it. Surely you jest.

Ate a pharmaceutical called 'the trollop's cure for female problems' the first time my name was called to the family way. The church condemns this form of abortifacient. I have sought forgiveness of my wayward will.

The Lord proved my womb fruitful, and the pill inactive. I produced such a marvelous child as Willie.

Cordially yours,

Isabel Mackenzie King

Suppose Isabel thought, 'Willie's secrets are not very well kept. Regrets. He's a good boy. I wanted a daughter.'

Geboren.

Um 17. Dezember, die Frau von John King in Berlin, einen Sohn.

"Faith of our Mothers, living yet
In cradle song and Bedtime prayer,
In nurs'ry love and fireside love,
Thy presence still pervades the air"

by ISABELLE FORSKYN

Mother, a name of honour given to a woman—and all mothers each in their own way give to their children their personal interpretation of honour. To-day when all our hearts are turning to the other who is ours, we give you Mrs. Isabel Grace Mackenzie King, the mother of the prime minister of Canada.

A favourite expression of Mrs. King's was, 'Knowledge is easily carried like the mail' i.e., to know how to accomplish many things is no added weight. Mrs. King taught her children to believe in the common fellowship of man, and that no discrimination should be made because of birth or position.

She watched three score and ten pass through Salvador's hourglasses. Stream along sides of eyes into their ears. He tossed time pieces to the ground.

Mrs. John King,

Your concern has been noted.

We, too, at Saint Paul's optimistically believe the new millennium will be wrought with ongoing successes in the field concerned with ailments of the mind. We are pasteurizing the universal medicine, panacea.

Diseases of excess, such as that which harms William King must be stopped. Whether it is through the finer points of living under the scalpel or in breeding we will succeed.

> ". . . thro' the ages one increasing purpose runs,
> And the thoughts of men are winden'd wit the process of the suns."

May William and you survive to walk the bridge into that country. We will herd him safely home. Oh, may you, Mrs. King hear.

Her biological clock spun .stopped

Of my warm wet-nurse:

Oddly, she has no navel. I take it from my chest, ma, she resembles you uncannily. It is as tho' she kneels over a stream admiring another Isabel below.

She, deaddog, lowered her mother tongue to lick me. My death bed. Dead letter.

I gasp in away as you appear to me here, in Kingsmere. My mother, rest upon your old stump & read to me from the sundial perched atop. Sundials you must know consist of two parts—the style or gnomon, usually the edge a plate of metal or a small rod, parallel wt. the axis of the earth; & the dial-face, in which are marked the numerals of the hours of the day.

All I see is an appealing scattering of your cumulonimbus hair running away wt. the wind. The sun seems to follow your face.

In heaven, greet my nurse & knock on wood once you have.

~~I cannot write~~
~~or spill vinegar~~
~~on these pages whl.~~ ~~i~~
~~age~~

~~a fly on the mirror~~
~~mirror on the wall~~
~~flower.~~

Where three roads meet, I sing on my two feet.

born
on iv legs

a parable of error
pair this able
soul with M.

I read left to dead to rights.

Bedridden I wallow
in ashen sheets.

Aflame, I dreamed -
I see in her eat a
puss
'n knock boots
scent of dink
& wrinkled leather boot
stink.

I profess,
wt. sunken cheeks
self abuse (~~Bt.~~
~~me willie shall reign~~
~~where're the son~~)

no other love like

Nurse maid,

I pray for a cessation of Willie's wanton ways. He has indeed mentioned interest in the 'delightful nurses' he engages wt. He intends to follow one (M.) to Chicago once his treatment has run its course. May he cast her nation of unborn children into the great lake of forgetfulness. I beg him to make quick work of it. I pray he has the strength of his namesake, rebel William.

‘Backward turn backward’. Softly
Interned wt. thee, & me. We were
Weary, & we, we cried ‘Oh Faith
Ful Shepard’. Too-da-loo, I ~~lay~~ lie
In ~~feces~~ waste. Before, teeny weeny boy at play,
I saw thee, Mother, singing sad
Ly. But *oh!*
Die. A hard-on fallen.

Isabel,
he may not overcome the darkness for he who pens this is not he at all she is

M.

In censoring your son’s correspondence, we have found he is unaware of his mistaken conception and miraculous birth.

We have consulted with a Doctor (~~we shall name him John~~) and he recommends I end my pregnancy. We’re not even sure it’s a baby.

(Handwritten)

Today manna seems to have fallen again from Heaven. The morning mail brought much more than words can begin to express, and all coming just at this time makes it precious, priceless. I am sure that it is all evidence of a divine providence, and plan - indeed within itself—with the chain—charmed circle of communication there is so much to indicate.

envelope nineteeneighteen

willie pissed in me i a mother of illegitimacy chew (you)rself
out of fishnet

did not de-sire to keep my malformed manchild--an oyster shucked
likened unto a toad--that squat person
(you)ll find it drowned

Incident of Infanticide.

M. P. King, well-aged, resided wt. his mother, deceased, suddenly. The following facts were elicited in a correspondence wt. a nurse-maid.

He died on——, after nine bawdy months of gestation, at the age of nothing. His mother had worked at Saint Paul's for about fifteen years before her trouble. She was admitted to her own hospital in the summer of 1918, & was under the care of Dr. ——, of —— . She had all her teeth extracted & portions of her jawbone removed. Was confined to bed for five months & endured terrible suffering from the ulceration of the jaw & decay of the bone. In describing the cause of her death, the expression used by one of the patients was, 'She died in childbirth, but she would have died of consumption inevitably, by swallowing pus from an ulcerated jaw.' The manchild born gagged wt. a baton head wrap around the underside of his jaw & top of head died immanently upon spill. It is a sin & a crime & is also wrong.

Interment followed, not a scattering.

accursive

ma lad rote:
Malady without
my lady. My
content abyss,
delicious &
unmaid.

the working of women at high
pressure should be made a crime
as law as it is a crime against
nature herself

Industry and Humanity p. 160

Letters opened her. Mailman read while squatting, peeing in bushes, watching Isabel. His sooty hand smudged these correspondences, thorns of smutty lovers.

<u>Friday, December 31, 1899.</u>

The spiritual beauty of this posey is to my mind passing grand: to see, as you soon will, what remains on the dark side of the glass. Once blinded, now I see! The postman is stamping my mother.

still as a morning gobble
plumbing drain
deep sewer dripping
mirroring king

i & i

Living clean in age
of plagues
(On
Victoria Day 1898
U.S. at
Canada Club
dinner):

in a king
sized bed
i

i
legs

core
us
playher
in-

I seek asylum
from this little
affliction.

trance &
continent

eggshit & pull & 'n &
mt. cuntry beautifully
that I thigh
enter & exhit&inher &
off&onno&on&noon ohno
&enter&eulalia uuu uu you
back & in

pulin' ot. in
u in
me
'n
time

c
o
M. e

(A go from my
good little
nurse in Chicago).

Rex. —Come mother, it's your séance. Mother, is it you?
Mrs. Wreidt. —Mother?
Mother. —Her.
R. —Can you tell me Mother, over this little table, am I mistaken?
M. —Kin?
R. —Was I mistaken?
Mrs. W. —Guess.
M. —Yes.
R. —Is this my inheritance? Am I forsaken?
Mrs. W. —Hands off, dummy!
R. —Stay!
M. —Stay. She has left me in spirit. Silent.
Mrs. W. —William?
R. —Yes.
Mrs. W. —You are a marionette.
R. —I will no longer carry you.
Mrs. W. —I heard someone. Is there someone, a herd nigh?
M. —I?
R. —Don't stiffen on me.
M. —Come.
R. —She waxed warm. Somewhere her spirit dwells, not far from me here.
Mrs. W. —Come.
R. —I'm coming, I'm com—me? ah!
Mrs. W. —We are members one of another.

Echoes only voice, no body; Mrs. pare ode from bone.
Under broken water, left naught. King clasps alone.

6 Dec. 1918

I see me in my silver spoon.

I am here gazing at your shrine. Five portraits of you peer down at me. Your memories escape.

I am on my way from Ottawa, please be there ’n spirit when I arrive. I feel that wiser old heads may help chicken scratch my memoirs. I, henpecked? Nuptials? Goose pimples! Not me, M. Magdalene.

Will you pat my head when I come? If not, we will walk to get her over the monument in the family cemetery bed. There. We will leave any further comment on the love making until we can talk together.

Male: King wed
his own M.
other
man & wife I fear
his paramour was more
of a poppycocktease.

I saw her
in rusty tub water
gobbling red
head horny
cuckold.

When the light
ning struck buckled
a divining rod.

IN THE SECOND SIGHT OF THE ALMIGHTY GOD

a revelation of things as they are

O vitæ Philosophia dux! O virtutum indagatrix, expultrixque vitiorum!
Cicero

TO THE MEMORY
OF MY FATHER

AND
MOTHER

OTTAWA. 1867 AND SO ON

'I was well, I wanted to be better, & here I am.'

When I hear of death there comes to mind an Italian epitaph which Sir John A. Macdonald was fond of quoting in his day. The above transcription is of one who sought change unnecessarily.

Set this down on the inner leaf of my memoirs.

W.L. Mackenzie King

Panel 1[fullpage]: Title,

CANADA'S KING

Panel 2 [inlaid]: Cane & hat in hand, King & his dog, an Irish Terrier, promenade on a maple leaf.

Cap [upon another leaf in the background]:
CANADA HAS A KING
& HIS NAME IS WILLIAM.
HEAD NORTH & YOU'RE IN
HIS KINGDOM

Panel 3: A boy bites another on the ankle at the intersection of dirt roads.

IN BERLIN (TRUE NAME!) CANADA IN !*&$,
KING WAS BORN WITH MANY NAMES:
WILLIAM LYON MACKENZIE.
SOMETIMES HE THOUGHT HE WAS
KING OF THE JUNGLE

Panel 4: King, braggadocio about town, with hat hidden in his frock coat and hands on his lap says:

LET ME LIVE HERE AND HELP YOU
HELP THE POOR, MARY.

Mary, wearing a blue petticoat, replies:

YOU DON'T HAVE ANY CHILDREN
DO YOU, YOUNG MAN?

WHAT IF THE KING DIES?
LONG LIVE THE—

Untrue Comics #1 January 1942.

Labour Day.
(Flearidden)

After breakfast, I listened to the King's speech, which I fancied very good. Shortly after, I sent a cable to the lord asking him to let the King know that His Majesty's broadcast came over perfectly. It was a well-worded broadcast.

If the King dies, he rises at dusk in the son.

ON AIR

By the wonderful development of radio broadcasting, we hope that the peal will be heard not only throughout our Dominion, but that it be carried also to the distant Empire. Sounding clear as pearl.

We know of King's mourning. King did not resurrect a corpsecadaver a duallydead *placenta even though her voice rang in his ear.*

Born still. Born again, in her womb he contracted congenital wounds. We wrote her immortal unborn into being. We can write it out. Mailman your pen and smear struck her mother's rigour ceases let you be the son to her homemaking moon.

Fill our hallowed lungs with air. *My err. Your ear.*

MY PLAN OF TEACHING.

PREPARATORY WORK: So far as I know I give the only course which starts the student out upon a plain common sense basis of taking subjects by channelling spirits. The principle practice for success is to possess. In plain, once you own a subject's possessions, you own the subject. Towards this end: I will cite a particular subject (for reasons of anonymity pen-named Rex), to be typical. My name remains Mrs. Wreidt, but I will abbreviate my name Mrs. W. Through our methods you commence with tests in which you will not channel actual spirits (yet you will sound as though you do). This is to ensure payment and the return of substance for your efforts. You would hardly be foolish enough to approach Rex, a stranger, and seek him to invite you to a home cooked meal in his village. If you wish to tea with Rex you will become intimately acquainted with him; you would win his trust and confidence; you would bring Rex step by step toward what it is he most constantly wishes. This is the proven and successful method.

LESSON 1.
IMPORTANT: IT IS IMPERATIVE THAT YOU LEARN EACH LESSON THROUGHLY BEFORE TAKING UP THE NEXT. Study each test in the order given. Do write me if you are in need of help, Mrs. W. is willing to reply (even personally, at your home), provided you have enclosed an addressed and stamped envelope.

Love costs fifty
salmoncoloured dollars
or, the cash
on hand to stare at
the RC's musical ride
mount & march in circles.

(we) mailmen cannot change an address addressee or orifice come
straight from the mare's mouth
bray riding shank her

King took Mrs. Wreidt, 'the best of all mediums', as his surrogate mother mortis. Did Isabel die in 1917 while the Canadian carillon tower blazed? The medium mimicked Isabel and hushed bells in her earrings mocked him.

I would tell you
the life of an old bachelor
(considers matrimony
to the last belle
he calls) is
a lonely life.

Ask mother
(my throat is vexed
sore) to burn all but
two of these
letters
(ruin & shatter
fifty-three bells pealing).
I meant to wed
(& I locked
me & ma to get her).

Fingers interwoven, she ignored his needling stub. Rex knelt before the little wooden table to baptize himself in her intrauterine river. He entered her and awoke her son.

"His kingdom spread from shore to shore,
'Till poets shall wax and wane no more."

On Mother's Day at Kingsmere, years later with Willy's remains we shared an elegiac parlance with Mrs. Wreidt. We grieved while King made a bride of our Isabel, mother. Descendants waded in diseamen.

Ye angels lie radiantly
Wt. us in chorus. On, to, one,
Two onto into the 'City
Of Dog'. Mother, thou wolds't not alone.

The Sunday School Lesson

Kingsmère—CHAPTER 10

9 Thy time is five after the seventh hour of Pat's passing. Pat knew my works and the war that kills the nation's children with the death; and all the churches will know my love for these my children. My angel flies as a dove straight from my hands rise unto the arms of Jesus.

8 Pat suffers no further ailments in this his seventeenth year. Behold the mirror of these eyes. He is my little angel dog that has become a dog angel this day. My love for Pat, my only child.

7 He that hath an ear hearken:

High up in the courts of Heaven to-day
A little dog-angel waits,
With the other angels he will not play,
But sits alone at the gates;
For I know that my master will come,
says he:
And when he comes he will call for me.

6 For Pat served to support me in this the most critical of moments. I cry as I realize that Pat's little spirit, his brave, noble spirit has taken its flight. But these shivering tears are mostly in gratitude for God's mercy in so guiding my steps as to bring me home to Kingsmère in time.

5 I write, remember therefore from whence thou art a fallen King, and repent, and do the first works as with the bells of heaven ringing. Or else I will come unto thee quickly in the form of a man setting a fiery eye to your evil letters.

4 Behold in the light of a candlestick at the little table what the spirit saith, in seance, unto the King; To him that overcometh will I give to eat of the vine of grapes, which is in the midst of the chorus of heaven here in the ruins of my village.

3 Behold I will hold my pen from thee, diary. It has given me space to repent of my wrong doings since the time in my youth that I was called Rex. I feel it is meant for me, a part of God's plan, for me to renounce for ever the use of alcohol.

2 I no longer desire to fill thee with my writings. Behold I cast thee upon the table, and them that commit selves to her in reading will suffer great tribulation, except those who repent.

1 Yet I have a few things against thee, because thou sufferest that malapert Isabel, which calleth herself my mother, to teach and to seduce my self and commit fornication, and to read things sacrificed to idols. I feel a great peace it has all ended.

ERRATA

Did not wait to read newspapers to-night. Turned out light; in bed 12.20. Little Pat was waiting for me in the mid-stairs hall, for my coming in at midnight.

King's Best Friend

By D. DONG

A dog house in heaven houses old Pat, the Prime Minister's beloved Irish terrier.

Pat once slept in a basket at Mr. King's feet, under his bed. Before bed, Pat's master baited him into the basket oh so carefully wrapping him with a shawl once belonging to his mother.

In the light of his caregiver's lonely peculiarity and occasional eccentricity, Pat was a friend completely intimate and deeply missed.

your letter september nineteenfortysix

I know what is right, Mother.

This is right you suck the breast that feeds you, but will he, you willy bite my bitch bosom. Wench, whelp. Kick you from my hind teat.

Titillating. My nipples harden & darken while thinking of telling. Irksome, penny sized, copper coloured, welts, fall. The letters, mail, & man stretch like an aged tattoo, or flush Braille.

I cannot complete my memoirs.

Whr. is my billy club? Decepter! She hid it. In one of those rank spoiled omelettes. Alabastard tissue.

I cannot see him whl. drawing Mrs W.'s bath. I spelunked your shrouded plot. I mine wealth. What is mine.

We will be Kings of Canada.

Sunday, December 4, 1938.

My wish in meeting the King is to complete the work of my grandfather & of Liberalism thus far in Canada, 1837-38 the struggle for freedom in Government - complete self Gov't (wanted by Mackenzie under the Crown). If I go to meet the King and am the first to welcome a British Sovereign to his 'Dominion' beyond the Seas, Canada being full-fledged nation, the cycle & the century wd. be complete. I believe in the providence of God this is ordained.

Willy Mackenzie, his grandfather, aroused a government to overthrow the British inbreds. Without weapons, Mackenzie called forth a bloody discharge in Toronto & was beaten back by bands of Loyalists.

My narrative begins in Upper Canada of the early nineteenth century. My grandfather William, the father of many Kings, grieved under his wife, who had used her social influence in placing herself among the ruling class of friends. She domineered & killed many of William's supporters as they sat after sundown. These supporters ran cold wt. the notion of responsible government. His wife's profits allowed her to search four hundred fifty, nearly all, of William's followers at the caves of Navy Island in the Niagara River. In 1838, these noble rebels had formed a provisional government of Upper Canada. William served to organize this responsible government & strived to carry out the vanquished wishes of the government & his rightly attained office. He had the people's support, but the owner of the ungodly womb vanquished his people. William could no longer represent otherworldly ghosts & drifted toward the border for solace whr. the new found land met the sky.

My grandfather remained loyal to his high ideals. He scolded his wife, left her, & began recruiting chargers however necessary for his next flight into Upper Canada. The narrative goes on to say that his family sat on the steps the night before, as had been their wont since their first days, & talked together in the evening's twilight. A veiled visitor came from the place of William's birth; he had known her as a boy, but had not seen her since. Believing that this old acquaintance must have some request to make, but was hesitant about preferring it, as he could not make ot. the identity of the elderly goody woman in rags. So grandfather sought to ease the situation by inquiring in the village Post office whether there was a vacancy that she would fill; whether she had relatives who vanquished commission in the rebel army, or whether some friend of hers had contacts in which she may also be interested. In vain did grandfather skulldig to determine that there was no ulterior motive in her visit. Finally, William said to her, 'then why did you come?'

To which his friend of earlier days replied, 'I came, Willie, to see you. I knew you would be anxious & worried wt. this battle. That you would have someone to talk to; I knew that at this time you would be glad to see one of these folks from home so I just came to see you'.

'You came to see William Mackenzie, & for no other reason!' spake William.

'Yes Willie, what other reason could I have?' & she removed her Sunday best.

It was too much for grandfather. I am told that William, whom all the terrors & responsibilities of a war could not shake, broke at this expression of disinterested, true-hearted friendship. Of all the people wt. whom William had conversed during the period of the war, yes, possibly of his lifetime, this woman had nothing to find, she had a great desire to share a burden, a great desire to burden.

Walking through Woodside, I gather facts beneath figures of Isabel King.

What is her great influence on her son? Sitting on his mother's knee, King was undoubtedly regaled of tales about her father, in light of his father's absence.

Later a government representative, King's indoctrination may have been stories of his grandfather's fight for representative government.

This was very likely the impetus behind King's name change. Early in life, William Lyon asked his friends to call him Mackenzie King.

* * *

THEREFORE a maternal grandfather complex made this king Oedipus complex.

Rex. —I was strolling with a well-known Ottawa lady through the streets of the capital before a great sheaf of letters an umbrella in my hand. She turned into a sort of hut or teepee in which men seemed to be lying in pajamas with their legs extended. Suddenly the word kanata came very strongly to me that it was the group who called themselves the ancient indian term for village, for our great nation. Trees felled & wheat planted. I pretended to stare at the men while I followed the woman with my eye. She was coy with my desires. The lady roused several men to take me away. I passed by, coughed for air, and they all slept. The men all faced the east. She stumbled and I fell over the lady. Quite a lass. I was sad when I felt close. I bent over, pulled the tails of a blouse under and through a top buttonhole. My senseless fingers found lint in her exposed belly. I entered, hollowed her den. She: 'Come?' Come. The night chill I awoke and threw off my brown quilt at once. My mind aroused, I despised my useless prick. I tucked myself back in.

Mrs. Wreidt. —Alas sweet boy beloved in vain.

R. —What? I, vain?

Mrs. W. —

R. —Mother, speak.

Mrs. W. —Other speak.

R. —Are you the one who is near to me. In dreams? Hour by hour?

Mrs. W. —Coeamus.

R. —What is in your tattling throat? The Medium's voice or yours?

Mrs. W. —Let us join.

R. —Would I rather die if you would not take pleasure in me.

Mrs. W. —Pleasure in me.

R. —You're cold.

Mrs. W. —Old.

requiem for pneumonia

bells rang   ting   tinambulation
my lady. Madness,   will M.urges
ceremony, King my   malleable hollow
hand enraptured   squidsquirtquills
inside her halo   holy in my hand
matrimony ring.   half-finger king
alarum urges.   circles the throne

wreidt is a bell   sounding
we ring in   *cannot look*
you in the face   *when we are talk*
ing, so its wright to   *ii have a mirror in*
our room. Between fem   *i mean Isabel, his mother.*
inane marriage vows m ise en scène, we're burying
ta
king.   *casket*
His belle   *babel lit &*
emerged a   *carillon*
virgin   *struck.*
. Dinging   *warning.*

vacuum
i return two double
youthere is
no (we)there is no we
there is no we
here youyoume
wee(gee
w e)
w
e
uu

w

e
w

EULOGY

Regaled a pillar covered in bedsores. An ennobled phallus. Ashtoreth. A will

I
am
the
king
w .Son
e &
jac mot
u her.
late Stroke
in a by
cest woe stroke
u ful
al
na
tion
of
male
wee wees
ran all the way home

We wee ones heed the King's phlegmatic final instructions, lest Rex returns to ruin his story. The Son King, a scourge. Our mail order bride.

Heliotropes drop ’twixt wealth and embers. I have not long to live.
The flower of youth dies. De-spite Isabel’s vaginal sieve.

Atop her little orphaned wooden table, Mrs. Wreidt, at King’s request,
communed with Isabel. The mailman took Isabel King’s name and
corresponded with King. We collected Willy’s legacy, his will to revive
her. Receive her. Conceive her. We write necromantically, having read
entrails. I was doing last night what brought so much trouble
reading readingdearly reidan bkroe dwon & siad not to raed .but
went on and your descriptive account became beautiful whr. were
you went to sleep atop mother with your story .You, dear mum
acquire the habitude of these virtues and I will try
to be more moral than my words & thoths (we)are isabels
postmortemnomduplu(me)

Mrs. W. —I here am lamenting; a sheared wood nymph in Hades.
Look how often I kissed you. You stooped with me, intermingled &
drank. I, an empty ladle. I raised the regicidead.

Rex. —This is not right. It is the lying spirit. Not mother.

KEEP THESE INSTRUCTIONS STRICTLY PRIVATE:

A correspondence course to become an effective Conversationalist,
Direct Voice Medium,
Spiritualist, etc. in séance by X. MRS. HENRIETTA WREIDT.

Copyrighted 1939, by the above for the use of deciphering events,
times, seasons, etc. & prophesy. All rights reserved.

N.B. Persons making copies of these instructions and the examples
thereof, will be held amendable to the law (those characters herein
are representative types. None is real).

AUTOBIOGRAPHY

Silence is lanced language. I broke the habit of
prattling, punning, & joking. Were it known, audiences would find
my reason flawed. A grey scalp gone spotty.

You revolt against 'spiri-
tualism' & all that ilk. All willy nillyness is outgrown. You have
attained the wisdom of my sweet little mother. The widow being
oppressed, the orphan wronged, the tirants raigne . . .

Through
imposture, foppery, moral ambiguity I desire to have made kept myself up to appearances.

Hear the secret: we hitched. Itcontractions our day period My time to bleed has come. A babe comma born clothed, cries until hoarse wt. this cunnilingual tongue. Prolifierate!

i dilate

LESSON 2.
SECOND TEST—USE OF THE HYPNOTIC RING
Be sure to explain to the subject that he must not resist. Many will resist you when they tell you otherwise. Kneel before him, as Mrs. W. does with Rex, and hold the ring five inches from his eyes, requesting him to look at the point of the chain to the ring. Hold the ring still for about half a minute, - longer for difficult cases, - and while holding it chant in slow and decided tones 'When—I—draw—this—ring—from—you,—you—will—follow—after—the—ring.' Now draw the ring very slowly from the subject (and Mrs. W dropped the ring in her lap), and if susceptible he will fall forward. Thus the hex is drawn. Thus the rex is—

I gave a ring.
ringringringringringringring
grin ring ing grin ing ring ing grin ing ring
ring ing grunt ing reaching inside her i write ring in grin
in her against her will: (i am not giving in) Her: 'no.' rings in er rrr r
r i ii i in nn nnnn err ring giving not nearly tearing g ggg nnn nn n n
ii

i i two kings possess wreidt's ring
running over wt.in her
around groin rim belle
groaning ot. songs of
cunt brazen i write
you reap her &
she gives a son
heir of your
damned
kingdom
as other
rows of
belles
ran
&
the
sun
rose

uneven pupils

MY GENERAL RESOLVES there is real strength

THE MORNING.		
Question. How may you		Ris , wash, shav ’v ry s cond
indoctrinate a release from the		day, & pray ‘God may guid
Dark ages?	5	choic & ord r all things to
		Your own b st nd’;
		mast r s lf, abus diary & l tt r.
	6	writing, & br akfast.
	7	
	8	Work & r st, li fallow & study
		& r ad & think.
	9	
	10	
	11	Count pounds, ov r look my
		accounts, & partak of daily
NOON.		br ad.
Advance on chaos & th	12	
dark.	1	Subdu prid . Disguis it,
		struggl wt. it, b at it down, stifl
	2	it, mortify it as much as pl as s
	3	sinc it is aliv & will p p ot. &
		show its lf.
	4	
	5	Supp r; ‘God b thank d who
		match d us wt. His hour’;
	6	daily affairs; l ctricity studi s.
EVENING.		What ls can I do? Circl sins.
Question. What chaos have	*7*	
you prevented today?		
	8	R ad, wail aloud; fail, suff r;
		s v r d sup rfluous l ft ring fing
	9	r at s cond knuckl;
		bl d, a chick n geek *with his*
	10	*h ad cut off.*
	11	

NIGHT 12 Li, rst.

1

2

3

4

THE MOURNING.

Question. Have you come the Divine Right of Kings? the gospel?

N. B. Can no longr asily typ'writ ltt'r E. Sorry.

CHAPTER 9

The death of Jezebel

37 And when Baal was come to
Jezebel, he painted her face like
that of Write, and tied her head,
and looked out a window.

36 And as Baal entered in at the
gate, he lifted his face to the win-
dow, and said, Is this the womb
that carried children and self? Is
this the belle who lay with Rex
and had lain with Baal in the
hour of temptation? Is this the
one with child?

35 And Jezebel answereth, I
have not born any children. For
they are wicked monsters and I
smite them down as a eunuch, or
malamute.

34 And Baal said unto Write, who rose from the place where she was nearly slain, Throw her down. So she threw Jezebel the mother down and some of her blood was sprinkled on the table, and on the vine and Baal trod her underfoot.

33 And Write went to speak of Baal unto her: but she found no more than her ribs, and her teeth, and the flats of her thighs. Thus Baal's words had been spake true that dogs shall eat the flesh of Jezebel.

32 And Rex returned to the very place of he who bore him, son and husband. The very same table where he came to his mother, wet with Jezebel's blood. And he was exceedingly afraid as knelt hearing Write's song.

31 And he espied the carcasse of Jezebel and saith, This is not a wife or mother. Rex plucked out his eyes in mourning and saith, I shall remain in and wed this house forever as king mourning no children and call this place Kingsmother. And I will write of this house, throne, and tell of the lineage. We are one once more: mother and child.

30 Where is the prince?

a letter you did not send

I feel so barren wt. ot. a family of my own. My heart yearns for you. God grant I may return soon.

I question my very voice. Whr. did this hollow ringing come from? [word illegible] Your passing has left my maw ajar for no one.

I need a son. I need a King. I am wt. ot. an heir.

Hair only ventures forth whr. the body intersects. I intermingle King & King weaving me & me, me & you. Snatched spiral wreath.

Do I exaggerate the significance of a perfectly natural phenomenon. Am I listening to a mere spectre? Is there danger in a healthy man who misses you? [word illegible],

Wee Willie Winkie
Ran Through The Town
Up Stairs & Down Stairs
In His Night Gown

[~~Apologies for such pocked penmanship.~~ ~~My three-headed mangy mongrelled dog bit my mangled hand.~~ ~~I write this not of my own will~~ word illegible .]

burn
this
shit
&
kitty
hairs
misshis
wr ight
sun f ll
twit twat
piss burn
you moan i
s lf i ll abus
littl willy M.
h ir h a ballad
rap was wright
M. bar ass stroll
my phallus f ll damn
burns ov r wt. in h r
c l   r as a b ll   ill will di
r r ng g in nn nnbb bb burn this mouthing ringing sin u uuu nnn
n in h r an us p nis we: (not my willi h irs) B ll s: 'y s.' h burns in
burn ing burn this offspring insid h r i writ sham ing in burn
burn v ning grin ing burn ing burn t hiss miss
burnthisburnthisburnthisburn
Erron ous syphilis.

king's(mère) A You Too Biography

seventeen dec eighteenseventyfour born grandson of william lyon mackenzie rebel

eighteensixtyone death of william lyon mackenzie poor

1895 *Toronto. University of: B.A.; LL.B., 1896.; M.A., 1896.*

9 Mar. 1897 The Dr. thinks I have typhoid.

<u>October 12.</u>

Attended then a medical lecture on Venereal diseases in wh. the lecturer described syphilis its stages etc the room was filled with men, some had to leave during lecture & 2 fainted outright. It was most instructive tho' not attractive, a very necessary sort of lecture to be given to college students. It was a great lesson to many there tonight.

<u>September 7, 1901.</u>

I never knew Matthew Arnold before, I can never cease to love & reverence him now.

11 Jul. & 21 Sept. 1902 *No writing in diary.*

1913 *No writing in the diary.*

10 p.m. 3 Feb. 1916 *Parliament aflame, carillon silenced. Rebuilt 1927.*

twentyninth march nineteeneighteen   wrote first word about isabel kings death mt pleasant cemetery

1918   *Industry and Humanity*. TO THE MEMORY OF MY FATHER AND MY MOTHER.

1926   *Lost vote of confidence.* created old age pension

nineteentwentyone-nineteenthirty   prime minister

1928   *The Message of the Carillon.*

nineteenthirtyfive-nineteenfortyeight   prime minister (for twenty-two years)

1940.   *Last word on Pat.* Unemployment Insurance

1941   Pat dies. *Canada at Britain's Side.*

1944   *Canada and the Fight for Freedom*. family allowances act

Throughout the evening,
members of his personal staff as well as his Nurses,
were at Mr. King's bedside. The rain had then come on, and at
9:42 PM the group assembled in the little room to pray.
Kingsmere, Que.

CREDITS

"Mary & John" and "B - I - double" from *Mrs. King : the life and times of Isabel Mackenzie King* by Charlotte Gray. Toronto, Viking Penguin, 1997. Used with permission.

Nature and other Miscellanies (1836) by Emerson, Ralph Waldo. London: Oxford University Press, 1922.

Selected Poetry of Tennyson (1842) by Tennyson, Alfred Tennyson, Baron, Ed.

Douglas Bush. New York, The Modern Library/Random House, 1951.

Industry and humanity; a study in the principles underlying industrial reconstruction by King, William Lyon Mackenzie. Toronto, The Macmillan company of Canada Limited, 1935

The message of the carillon and other addresses by King, William Lyon Mackenzie. Toronto, Macmillan Company of Canada, c1927.

The secret of heroism : a memoir of Henry Albert Harper by King, William Lyon Mackenzie. New York; Toronto, Fleming H. Revell, c1906.

"Jesus Shall Reign Where'e the Sun" traditional hymn by Issac Watts, 1719.

"Faith of our Mother" traditional hymn by A.B. Patten, 1876

To hear the story as it should be told, consult (as I have) Joy E. Esberey's *Knight of the Holy Spirit: a study of William Lyon Mackenzie King* for a reading of King's oedipal issues. C.P. Stacey does a fine job of reading King's diaries in *A Very Double Life: the private world of Mackenzie King*. To get the names, places, and dates straight, see J.L. Granatstein's *W. L. Mackenzie King* and J.W. Pickersgill's *The Mackenzie King Record.* Many King resources exist (for now) on-line. On the Kitchener Public Library's digitized Mackenzie King collection find articles of 'The Kitchener-Waterloo Record' and correct the headlines and stories I've altered (for years Alex O. Potter wrote a column, "Let's Reminisce," which I've renamed "Hearken Back"; Henry Koch penned what becomes "King's Birthplace Rests in pieces"; "Had Pillow Fight" is H.L. Staebler's recollection and the testimony "I remember seeing him . . ." is that of the Daughter of Rev. W. A. Bradley qtd. by Potter) and The National Library of Canada's scans of the W. L. Mackenzie Diaries (Isabelle Forsyth wrote "Mother, a name", an article in the diaries; "King's Best Friend" was to Bruce Hutchison's). See Don Brittain's work to hear him quote Bruce Hutchison, "If we don't understand King, we don't understand ourselves".

Too often acknowledgements read like dropping, or, even worse, naming names. Too too often I haven't said thank you.

Family

David Paul Foster for you are David
Mark Sampson for readin', 'riting, & arthritic wit
The Moustache for the time & dirty pantomime
My Foster Family
These who read & said nice things
(those who said nasty things didn't make the cut),
Robert Smith
Robert Kroetsch
Alison Calder
Warren Cariou
David Arnason
Those who blurbed me with their vocabulary of flattery
Editor,
Dennis Cooley
& the many who Turn stones,
Todd Besant
Sharon Caseburg
Kelly Stifora